FORCES OF NATURE

Hurricanes

By S.L. Hamilton

Visit us at
www.abdopublishing.com

Published by ABDO Publishing Company, PO Box 398166, Minneapolis, MN 55439.
Copyright ©2012 by Abdo Consulting Group, Inc. International copyrights reserved in all
countries. No part of this book may be reproduced in any form without written permission
from the publisher. A&D Xtreme™ is a trademark and logo of ABDO Publishing Company.

Printed in the United States of America, North Mankato, Minnesota.
112011
012012

Editor: John Hamilton
Graphic Design: Sue Hamilton
Cover Design: John Hamilton
Cover Photo: Getty Images
Interior Photos: AP-pgs 8-9, 16-17, 18 & 29;
Corbis-pgs 11, 19, 20-21, 22-23, 24-25, & 26;
Getty Images-pgs 1, 4-5, 12-13, 14-15; Library of
Congress-pg 10; National Oceanic and Atmospheric
Administration (NOAA)-pgs 6 & 27;
Thinkstock-pgs 2-3, 6-7, 28, 30-31, & 32.

ABDO Booklinks
Web sites about Forces of Nature are featured on our Book Links pages.
These links are routinely monitored and updated to provide the
most current information available.
Web site: www.abdopublishing.com

Library of Congress Cataloging-in-Publication Data

Hamilton, Sue L., 1959-
 Hurricanes / S. L. Hamilton.
    p. cm. -- (Forces of nature)
 Includes bibliographical references and index.
 ISBN 978-1-61783-261-1 (alk. paper)
 1. Hurricanes--Juvenile literature. I. Title.
 QC944.2.H36 2012
 551.55'2--dc23
                    2011029672

Contents

Tropical Cyclone!

Hurricanes are huge storms with rotating wind speeds of more than 74 miles per hour (119 kph). Swirling across the warm waters of the tropics, these terrifying forces of nature blast ashore, causing destruction and even death.

XTREME FACT – Hurricanes are usually about 300 miles (483 km) wide, but may be as large as 400-500 miles (644-805 km).

Hurricane Dennis hits Key West, Florida, in July 2005.

The Science

A hurricane forms in warm areas of the ocean where there are large temperature differences between the water and the clouds. The clouds pull up moisture and warm air from the water's surface. This creates a column of fast-moving air. This may form into a "tropical storm." If the winds speed up, it becomes a hurricane.

The "eye" of a hurricane is an area of low pressure in the center of the storm. It is usually 20-30 miles (32-48 km) wide. In the eye, the winds are calm and the skies are clear.

HOW A HURRICANE FORMS

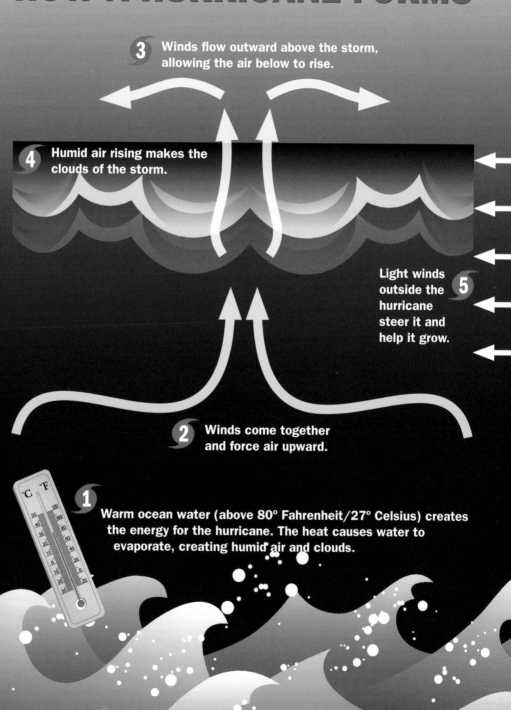

3 Winds flow outward above the storm, allowing the air below to rise.

4 Humid air rising makes the clouds of the storm.

5 Light winds outside the hurricane steer it and help it grow.

2 Winds come together and force air upward.

1 Warm ocean water (above 80° Fahrenheit/27° Celsius) creates the energy for the hurricane. The heat causes water to evaporate, creating humid air and clouds.

Hurricane Categories

Hurricanes are rated according to wind speeds. The United States uses the Saffir-Simpson Hurricane Scale. The scale ranges from a small category 1 up to a catastrophic category 5. But even the smallest hurricane can do terrible damage, depending on where it hits land, and how long it stays.

Hurricanes will become more destructive

Fewer but more ferocious and destructive hurricanes are likely to occur in the next century as a result of global warming. The most violent storms are expected to be concentrated in the west Atlantic, putting the Bahamas and southeast coast of the US at risk.

Saffir-Simpson hurricane scale

Category Four and Five storms doubled in frequency by the end of the 21st century

Wind mph	74-95	96-110	111-130	131-155	Over 155
Storm surge in feet	4-5	6-8	9-12	13-16	Over 18

Category 1	Category 2	Category 3	Category 4	Category 5
Minimal: No real structural damage some flooding	**Moderate:** Some roofing, material damage to buildings, small craft break moorings	**Extensive:** Structural damage to small houses and outbuildings, inland flooding	**Extreme:** Major structural damage, heavy flooding. Massive evacuation required	**Catastrophic:** Complete building failure, major damage, small structures blown over or away

Category Three to Five storms have accounted for 86% of all damage in the US caused by hurricanes

A United States Navy plane flies above the eye of a hurricane.

Historic Hurricanes

For thousands of years, hurricanes have turned coastal cities into areas of destruction. Some storms have been so terrible, they will never be forgotten.

GALVESTON HURRICANE - 1900

On September 8, 1900, the people of Galveston, Texas, became the victims of an evening hurricane that brought raging winds and huge waves of water. More than 8,000 people were killed and the town was destroyed.

XTREME FACT – In 1900, Cuban forecasters warned Texas that a hurricane was coming. Galveston officials did not believe them. No early warnings went out. Because of this, it became the deadliest hurricane to ever hit the U.S.

FLORIDA KEYS HURRICANE - 1935

On September 2, 1935, a category 5 hurricane struck the Florida Keys. Although there are no exact measurements, it is believed to have had winds of 150-200 miles per hour (241-322 kph). These violent winds, mixed with high tides, caused terrible destruction and 409 deaths. Many of the dead were World War I veterans who had been given jobs in the area. For days, little help arrived. The railroad line, the main means of transportation across the islands, was destroyed.

A train derailed by the 1935 hurricane near Islamorada, Florida.

Men search the rubble for victims of the 1935 Florida Keys Hurricane.

11

Infamous Hurricanes

A hurricane is a terror in open water, but when it hits land it becomes infamous. Modern warning systems and hurricane-proof buildings are not enough to stop a hurricane's destruction. Blasting winds, violent rain, towering waves, and severe flooding have made some hurricanes' landfalls both deadly and costly.

Hurricane Irene sends sea foam flying as it approaches Ocean City, Maryland, on August 27, 2011.

XTREME FACT – A hurricane can be called by different terms. If it forms in the North Atlantic or the Caribbean Sea, it is called a hurricane. If it starts in the Indian Ocean, it is called a cyclone. If it begins in the Pacific Ocean, it is called a typhoon.

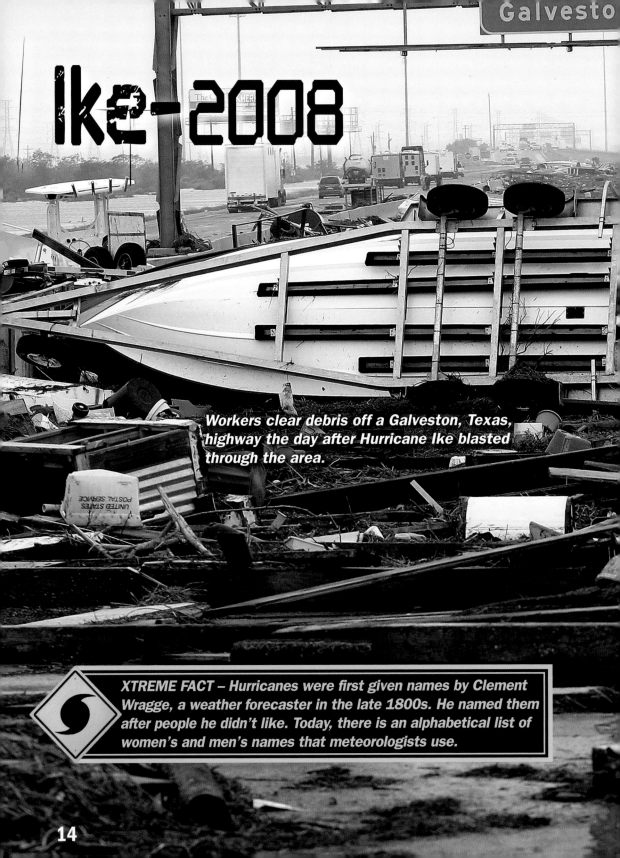

Ike-2008

Galvesto

Workers clear debris off a Galveston, Texas, highway the day after Hurricane Ike blasted through the area.

XTREME FACT – Hurricanes were first given names by Clement Wragge, a weather forecaster in the late 1800s. He named them after people he didn't like. Today, there is an alphabetical list of women's and men's names that meteorologists use.

On September 12, 2008, Texas was hit by Hurricane Ike. The category 2 hurricane created a storm surge that lifted water levels 10-15 feet (3-4.6 m). Flooding and winds caused 195 deaths and nearly $25 billion in damages. Ike was the third-costliest hurricane to hit the United States.

Katrina-2005

Strong winds from Hurricane Katrina blow the roof off a Louisiana restaurant on August 29, 2005.

Hurricane Katrina blasted the southern coast of the United States in August 2005. It struck Florida as a category 1 storm. But as it moved across the Gulf of Mexico, it gained strength, hitting Mississippi, Louisiana, and Texas as a category 3. The winds, rain, and flooding caused $81 billion in damages, and killed 1,836 people.

XTREME FACT – Hurricane Katrina was the costliest natural disaster in the history of the United States. It was also one of the five deadliest hurricanes in U.S. history.

Rita-2005

Hurricane Rita struck Texas and Louisiana less than a month after Hurricane Katrina. Rita made landfall on September 24, 2005, as a powerful category 5. People were told to leave, and they did. More than 2,700,000 people drove inland to safety. Rita caused seven deaths, and added to the destruction along the Gulf Coast.

Hurricane Rita strikes the already damaged New Canal Lighthouse near New Orleans, Louisiana, in September 2005. The lighthouse was completely destroyed after Rita went through, although efforts are being made to restore it.

Wilma-2005

Hurricane Wilma blasts Miami Beach, Florida, on October 24, 2005.

In the open ocean, Hurricane Wilma grew into the Atlantic's strongest storm of all time. When it hit Florida on October 24, 2005, Wilma had dropped to a category 3 hurricane. Wilma's 125 miles per hour (201 kph) winds caused more than $20 billion in damages. Much of Florida's orange crops were wiped out. Hurricane Wilma caused 62 deaths.

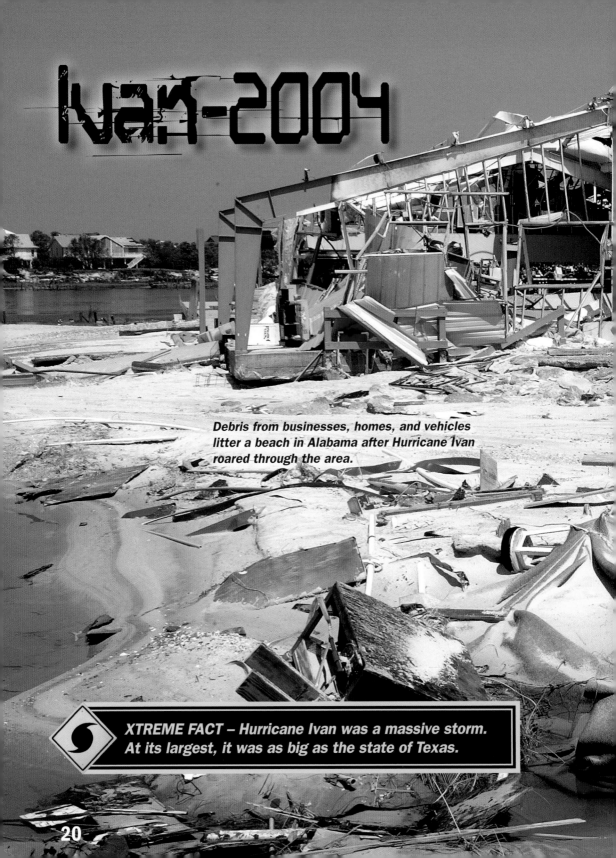

Ivan-2004

Debris from businesses, homes, and vehicles litter a beach in Alabama after Hurricane Ivan roared through the area.

XTREME FACT – Hurricane Ivan was a massive storm. At its largest, it was as big as the state of Texas.

Hurricane Ivan formed September 2, 2004, growing into a huge storm with category 5 winds. It weakened, but still hit Alabama as a category 3 hurricane on September 16, 2004. Heavy rains and wind caused more than $18 billion in damages.

Floyd-1999

A home on Oak Island, North Carolina, once on stilts, sits ready to wash out to sea after Hurricane Floyd struck it.

Hurricane Floyd struck North Carolina as a category 2 hurricane on September 16, 1999. Floyd dropped 15-20 inches (38-51 cm) of rain on the eastern part of the state. Two weeks earlier, Tropical Storm Dennis had already dropped huge amounts of rain on the area. Rivers and streams overflowed, causing massive flooding. Thousands of homes and crops were destroyed and 57 people died.

XTREME FACT – About 90 percent of hurricane deaths are caused by people drowning in the resulting floods.

Andrew-1992

Andrew hit southeast Florida as a category 5 hurricane on August 24, 1992. With winds of 165 miles per hour (266 kph), its destruction was catastrophic. Homestead, Florida, was reduced to rubble. Andrew was one of the costliest hurricanes to hit the United States, with more than $26 billion in damages.

A resident of Homestead, Florida, searches for anything left after Hurricane Andrew destroyed his home.

A person seeks shelter as Hurricane Andrew hits Florida.

Hugo-1989

Hurricane Hugo struck several Caribbean islands before making landfall in South Carolina in September 1989 as a category 4 hurricane. Its heavy winds and rain caused $9 billion in damages, and 49 deaths.

Hurricane Hugo blew ships into a stack on an island near Charleston, South Carolina.

Camille-1969

Hurricane Camille is one of the worst hurricanes to ever strike the United States. Smashing into the Mississippi coast on August 17, 1969, Camille brought 120-190 mph (193-306 kph) winds. Together with heavy rain, its path of destruction was horrific.

A destroyed area of Biloxi, Mississippi, in August 1969.

BEFORE

AFTER

A historic home in Mississippi was destroyed by the high winds and storm surge of Hurricane Camille. All that remained was the home's front steps (red arrows).

Surviving a' Hurricane

To survive a hurricane, it is important to know where to go and what to do ahead of time. Have a disaster pack ready with water, food, and medicines for at least a week. Keep flashlights and a weather radio available. Listen to all updates, and follow instructions from weather officials. If you are told to leave, know the evacuation route to take to get out. Being prepared saves lives.

A hurricane WATCH is issued when there is a threat of hurricane conditions within 24 to 36 hours. People should bring in any loose items in their yards and secure windows and doors. They should then stay inside.

A hurricane WARNING is issued when hurricane conditions are expected in 24 hours or less. If people are told to leave the area, they should make sure their cars have full gas tanks, then evacuate immediately.

In August 2004, people follow an evacuation route in Tampa, Florida, after being warned that Hurricane Charley was headed for their area.

Glossary

CATASTROPHIC
Great danger that is often sudden or unexpected, which typically leads to losses of life and property.

CYCLONE
A term for a hurricane that forms in the Indian Ocean.

DEBRIS
Pieces of objects that have been broken and scattered.

EVACUATION
An order to leave an area if that place is expected to become too dangerous for people to survive. When severe hurricanes are predicted, officials may announce evacuation orders. People are told to leave their homes and move inland to a safer location.

INFAMOUS
Well known for being particularly harsh or bad.

LANDFALL
When a hurricane hits land. Without the warm waters to keep it going, a hurricane will weaken once it makes landfall. However, it may take many hours for a hurricane to die out. A hurricane may also make landfall, move back out to sea, become stronger, and strike another area.

Meteorologist
A person who studies and predicts the weather.

Saffir-Simpson Hurricane Scale
A scale that classifies hurricanes according to their wind speeds. This scale was created in 1971 by Herbert Saffir, a civil engineer, and Bob Simpson, a meteorologist. The Saffir-Simpson scale is mainly used on hurricanes that form in the Atlantic Ocean and Caribbean Sea. Other scales are used in other parts of the world.

Storm Surge
When ocean waters suddenly rise to much greater-than-normal heights and flow far inland. A storm surge is usually caused by a hurricane's winds pushing on the ocean's surface. A hurricane-created storm surge often causes severe and deadly flooding.

Tropical Storm
A large mass of thunderstorms with circling winds of 39-73 miles per hour (63-117 kph). If the wind speed increases, a tropical storm forms into a hurricane.

Tropics
An area with year-round warm, humid temperatures. The tropics are approximately 1,630 miles (2,623 km) above and below Earth's equator.

Typhoon
A term for a hurricane that forms in the Pacific Ocean.

Index